Cradock Newton

A Rhymer's Wallet

Cradock Newton

A Rhymer's Wallet

ISBN/EAN: 9783337017002

Printed in Europe, USA, Canada, Australia, Japan

Cover: Foto ©ninafisch / pixelio.de

More available books at **www.hansebooks.com**

BY

CRADOCK NEWTON,

AUTHOR OF

"Arnold, a Dramatic History."

LONDON:
ALFRED W. BENNETT, 5, BISHOPSGATE WITHOUT.
1867.

UNWIN BROTHERS, PRINTERS, BUCKLERSBURY, LONDON, E.C.

CONTENTS.

	PAGE
Suspiria	1

SUGGESTIONS IN VERSE.

Mater Doloris	5
Philedonia	7
Wonderland	9
Lurleifelsen	13
A Pilgrim Stave	21
The Three Goblets	25
Lying in State	28
The Wonder-Flower	33
Bird and Bard	37
Hic Jacet	39
A Meditation	41
The Wishing-Bridge	43

LYRICS OF LOVE AND DEATH, ETC.

	PAGE
Olaf's Guests	47
Jarl Haldor's Daughter	49
Dead Minna	54
Edwin to Angelina	57
The Lover's Message	62
Barnewood Bells	64
Dora Herbert	66
Three Kisses	71
Ida's Gift	73
The Laurel Crown	75
A Shooting Star, observed from the Sea	77
The Final Blow	79
In the Spring	81
The Wayside Shrine	84
Jezer Horra	91

POEMS OF DISILLUSION.

The Amphitheatre	99
Disillusion	102
After-Dinner Talk	105
The Devil and Doctor Faustus	113
The Jester's Song	117

POEMS IN BLANK VERSE.

	PAGE
Sir Lancelot at the Cross	121
Pilate in Exile	128
The New Evangel	133
Anarchia	140

SONNETS.

Behind the Veil	149
Renunciation	150
Rejuvenescence	151
Sunset from the Cotswolds	152
Music from the Valley	153
The Italian Revolution	154
Excelsior	155
Failure	156
The Incomplete	157
Aspiration	158

SUSPIRIA.

When Life weeps solemn tears o'er Love's vain wrack,
When Faith the soul hath fled the corse of Form,
When all our wing'd desires are beaten back
Like wearied birds that buffet with the storm;—

When failing sights leave only strength to see
A doubt of all we hope and all we know,
Uprising as a dark funereal tree
'Gainst the grey gleam that follows sunset's glow—

Aid us, O God! Nor leave us yet to stand
In grosser regions, blind, unblest, undone,
But lift us to Thine holy table-land,
Where they that know and they that love are one:

Or, failing all, find grace the fate to bear—
As flowers from seeds chance-sown in caves of night,
That on their stinted dole of dismal air
Strive to fulfil their beauty, lacking light.

SUGGESTIONS IN VERSE.

MATER DOLORIS.

The embers are ashen, the shades down close—
And out of the shadows she grows and grows;

Her beauty is that of the dead, and her eyes
Are as angels' that weep for a lost Paradise;

In folds of dark sackcloth her figure is drest,
Round her brow is a thorn wreath, a cross at her breast;

And the voice of her singing is solemn and low,
Like the dirge of a joy that is dead long ago;

And the song that she sings is a song that seems
To wail for the lost in weary dreams;

The flow'rs that she bears are no blooms of pride,
She drops them to die where a past hath died;

The path that she leads is no path of bliss,
And tears are the fruit of her quiet kiss;

She leads to a grave which the sere leaves shroud,
And the night o'ershadows with cloud on cloud.

PHILEDONIA.

The robe she wears is like violet wine,
Whose soft lights lie on a soul of shade—
Divine she seems, yet is not divine,
So fair are the fallen angels made—
So fair are the passionate fallen made.

Her faint fierce glamour of touch and of eye,
The cruel warm sweet bane of her breath—
Love hath tasted these and must die;
What is left unto Love but death?—
The shrivel'd dust of a rose's death.

So from the dark to the dawn of day
A sorrowing angel sits, and sings
That the soul she hath lured with her lips of clay
Shall lose the wonderful gift of wings,—
The wonderful gift of heav'nward wings.

WONDERLAND.

Mournfully list'ning to the waves' strange voice,
And marking with a dim and moisten'd eye
The summer days sink down behind the sea—
Sink down beneath the brine, and slowly fall
Into the Hades of forgotten things;—
A mighty longing stealeth o'er the soul
As of a man who pineth to behold
Through parted years and pain on alien shores
One—all his memory, marvelling if her eyes
Live with the old love in them. Even so,
With passion strong as love and deep as death
Yearneth the spirit after Wonderland.

Ah, happy, happy land! The busy soul
Calls up in pictures of the half-shut eye
Thy shores of splendour, as a sad blind girl,
Who thinks the roses must be beautiful
But cannot see their beauty. Olden tones
Borne on the bosom of the breeze from far,—
Angels that came to the young heart in dreams—
In dreams, and dim and fair with forms of dreams
Return. The rugged steersman at the wheel
Softens into a cloudy shape, the sails
Move to a music of their own. Brave bark,
Speed well and bear us unto Wonderland!

Leave far behind thee the vext earth, where men
Spend their dark days in weaving their own shrouds,
And fraud and wrong are crowned kings, and toil
Hath chains for hire ; and all creation groans—
Crying in its great bitterness to God ;
And Love can never speak the thing it feels,

Or save the thing it loves—is succourless;
For whilst one saith, " I love thee," the beloved
Travelleth as a doom'd lamb the road of death,
And kisses fade so fast from lips that fade—
And garlands for the brow but green the grave,—
Roll, weary seas, ashore to Wonderland!

There larger natures sport themselves at ease
'Neath kindlier suns that nurture fairer flow'rs,
And richer harvests billow in the vales,
And passionate kisses fall on fadeless brows
As summer rain ; nor ever know they there
The passion that is desolation's prey—
The bitter tears begotten of farewells—
Farewells—nor meetings pale with parting's pain ;
For life is more than life, and love than love,
And, fed with sight serener, soul than soul.
Fair shore, unhaunted by impossible change,
Shine forth ! Waft, tardy winds, to Wonderland !

Alas! the rugged steersman at the wheel
Comes back again to vision. The hoarse sea
Speaketh from its great heart of discontent;
And in the misty distance dies away
The Wonderland—'tis past and gone. O Soul!
Whilst yet unbodied thou didst summer there,
God saw thee—led thee, lingering, forth with fear—
And sold thee in the Egypt of the sense,
And set the desert 'twixt thee and thy dreams;—
Yet with thy task-work thy deliverance win;
Believe and wait, and it may be that He
Will guide thee back again to Wonderland!

LURLEIFELSEN.

The smoke of the steamboat's funnel soileth the
 clear blue air,
Like the smear of a sooty finger daub'd o'er a picture
 fair ;

And the tourist grips his guide-book, and sneers
 with a passing sneer
At the foolish ancient legend of the whirling dark
 Gewirre;

But I sit ashore in the shadow watching the torrent strong,

And to me the Lurley, the Lurley, singeth the whole day long :—

" Come to me hitherward, downward ; deep as the heart of dreams—

Safe in a calm, unstirr'd by the swirl of the sounding streams,

" Lieth my rosy cavern, soft are its mosses sheen—

Soft is my couch of pleasure, my breast is the breast of a Queen !

" Wrapt in mine arms of quiet, lipp'd with my lips of love,

Thou shalt forget the ways and the woes of the world above ;

" The souls of the world above wander a wailing
  crowd—
Each with a shroud around him, each with a worm
  in the shroud.

" Will any earthly maiden soothe thee with kiss so
  sweet,
Or bathe with the milk of healing thy brow and
  thy burning feet ?

" Passion is pain and peril, and slayeth peace with a
  breath ;
Love is the rose of a day, whose root and rest are
  in death !

" Thou castest thine arms round shadows that vex
  thee, afar removed ;
Say if that which thou hast is as that thou hadst
  loved ?

" Thou seekest and findest never, and wanderest near
and far ;
Fortune and love flee from thee, child of an evil
star !

" Come to me hitherward, downward, mine are the
arms for thee ;
And there is a music of rest that is murmur'd by
none but me.

" For the peace that ceaseth strife, and stills desire,
are mine,
And I mingle sleep and death to a sweet and
soothing wine ;

" I will seal thy lips with silence, and touch thy brow
with balm,
And teach thee slumber's secret, and the happy soul
of calm :

" I will draw thy passion from thee, draw it from
 breast and brain,
I will breathe my breath upon thee and heal the
 pulse of pain ;—

" Thine heart shall yearn no longer for an earthly
 maiden's breast,
But thou shalt love the Lurley, and her cave and
 couch of rest.

" I know thine idle longings, and the wasted prayers
 I know
Thou hast sighed to the far and starry nights of
 the long-ago ;

" Madly aspires the spirit, mounting on broken
 wings,
And a mighty sorrow is born of the lore of lofty
 things.

" The bird, though it soar in ether, dies where it drew its birth;
The arrow shot at the sun comes heavily back to earth.

" What are the gains of wisdom, that only with toil befall
When the head is grey, and the heart is cold, and the world is all?

" Wherefore hunger for knowledge? Yea, though divine the lust,
'Tis a fantasy born in dreams only to end in dust.

" When thou hast conquer'd all with labour and toil of breath—
Lo! thy conquerors wait thee—these are they, pain and death!

" Come to me, hitherward, downward, to my cave
and couch below—
I will teach thee in one sweet whisper all that thy
soul can know ;—

" I have a kiss for the brow and the lips, and I lay
a touch on the eyes,
That shall make thee as wise as all that have lived
and learn'd and were wise !

" Come to me hitherward, downward—deep as the
heart of dreams,
Safe in a calm unstirr'd by the swirl of the sounding
streams,

" Lieth my rosy cavern, soft are its mosses sheen—
Soft is my couch of pleasure, my breast is the
breast of a Queen ! "

So, as I sit in the shadow, watching the torrent strong
To me the Lurley, the Lurley, singeth the whole day long.

A PILGRIM STAVE.

Forward ! in footstep together—
Cheerly, ere noontide be gone ;
Night, when the pilgrim is weary,—
Night and the end cometh on.

Marching in legion on legion,
Following legions pass'd o'er—
Martyrs, confessors, apostles,
Sages and saints gone before.

Many must fall by the wayside—
Wearily sink from the tread;
Weep them, but wait not in weeping;—
Leave thou the dead to the dead.

Here sinks the ruler, down-stricken,—
There quits the miser his hoard,—
Here sleeps the bard 'neath the daisies,—
The fighter is there with his sword.

Still the march moveth and moveth,
Thousands on thousands we press,—
Singing the same song and tending
On to the same goal no less.

Look not behind, lest thou sorrow—
See there thy youth's cherish'd worth,
Flow'rs of the garden of Eden
Trod 'neath the dust of the earth.

Wayfarer, wherefore be gazing
Back o'er the past of thy years,—
Where in the mist-closing distance
Veil'd stands the Angel of Tears?

Whoso will wait by the wayside
Falters and fails of the goal:
Thought is the palsy of purpose,
Action is hope for the soul.

Hark! through the soft summer stillness—
Hark! through the hush and the calm—
Voices for ever and ever
Chorus the world's marching psalm!

Pilgrim, be glad in thy nature—
Forward in step to the stave;
Taking the road through the valley,
Treading the road to the grave.

Half of the heights yet unmounted—
Half of the soul's strength to spare;
Rest shall await thee when weary,
Night with a morn otherwhere.

THE THREE GOBLETS.

" HERE is a rest for the weary,
　Here faith and patience be!
　But far in the wood by the wayside
　There wait Night's children three.

" Each holdeth a juice-fill'd goblet,
　Whose subtle lights shimmer and shine
　Like gems of the deep, deep ocean,
　Or jewels far in the mine.

"To the lips they are first as nectar,
　But ere one the taste repeat,
He shall say, 'These draughts of sweetness,
　Methinks they are bitter-sweet!'

"For who taketh the first fair proffer
　From him his faith shall flee,—
Who tasteth the cup of the second,
　His hope shall cease to be;
But who drinketh the draught of the Night's dark wine
　His heart's-love loseth he."

But he kiss'd her lips with laughter,
　And rode down the leaf-glade long,
Where through come the moan and the murmur
　Of the sister-sirens' song:—

"Ah, art thou athirst, Belovèd?
What juice like the juice I fill;
Drink till thou dream, and dreaming,
Quaff from the goblet still.

"Ah, hast thou been faint, Belovèd,
The perilous draught to drain?
Hither I bring thee healing,
Take, and be blest again.

"Ah, art thou then *mad*, Belovèd?
What opiate soothes like mine?
Tarry and drown thy fever
In drowsing and murmuring wine."

Stricken and sad returning,
When the sunset gleam was o'er
He looked on the face of the maiden,
And knew that he loved no more.

LYING IN STATE.

Ho ! World, whither hurriest ?   Stay !
Why so quickly away ?
And canst thou not watch by the side
Of this king in his pride—
One hour, ere the face-cloth be spread
O'er the face of the dead ?

" This king,"—lo ! what throne have we here ?
Bare walls and a bier ;
What ruled he or wrought that we bow
To crown him king now ?

His song or his thought had no pow'r
To take captive the hour;—
His wisdom won neither the state
Nor the wealth that make great.
At best, to our fancy he seems
But a dreamer of dreams.

"A dreamer,"—e'en so, yet 'tis true
What he dream'd thou shalt do;
All he fail'd in shall yet be fulfill'd,
All he censured be still'd;
The future that acteth his thought
Shall be honour'd unsought;—
Thyself shalt with splendour and speed
Crown the dream in the deed;—
Thyself shalt with noise of acclaim
Raise the doer to fame;—
While God to this dreamer shall say—
"Behold now thy day,

This work of thy thought was too true
For thine own day to do;—
Let others take praise in thy place,—
Gaze thou on My face."

So wrought he, content, who now seems
But a dreamer of dreams;
While the lusters for wealth or for pow'r
Sold their souls to the hour,
The lusters for pleasure sought bliss
In a cup or a kiss;
The pedant quenched truth with his prate;
The man of the state,
Clinging fast to fate's chariot strong,
Thought he guided along:
The priest, with his tithe-book for psalter,
Rang coin on the altar;
The sophist made wrong for right speak;
The demagogue sleek

Taught the slave-chain without was the sin,
Not the slave-soul within ;—
While each thou didst set on his throne,
This dreamer alone,
Unmindful to scheme or to bend,
Went unthroned to the end.

How lived he—this man above men,
Sphered so high o'er our ken ?
Was he pure as the stars ?   Did he fall,
Though so great, like the small ?
Strong in thought, weak in will,—thus did he
Fail even as we ?

World ! how shall I hope to sustain him
When thou dost arraign him ?—
There he lies, howsoe'er the vote fall,
Mute enough to it all.

See, he learns the great secret with grace

And composure of face,

As though, whate'er Heav'n grants or denies him,

No fate could surprise him.

'Fore what tribune would'st cite him for trial ?

He seems to defy all.

He appeals e'en *from* Cæsar.   So let him.

Pass on and forget him.

THE WONDER-FLOWER.

Adown the mountain's castled side
The shining meads spread far and wide;

There forth they crowd from town and tower
To seek the magic Wonder-flower;

The simple blossoms, meek and sweet,
Of spring they tread beneath their feet,

And pass them with an eager mind,
Intent the Wonder-flower to find.

Who finds it in its sheeny pride,
Wins every blissful wish beside.

The maiden seeks, that she may know
The love that makes a heaven below.

The young man seeks, with joyful hope,
That he may fill his soul's large scope.

The scholar seeks, with dreamy eyes,
That he to hidden lore may rise.

The miser seeks, his painful store
Perchance to swell from more to more.

All seek, and seek till life grows grey,
But none hath found it to this day;—

Yet fondly fashioned tales are told
Of those who sought and found of old,

In songs that ancient women weave,
Youth's credulous ardour to deceive.

So forth the streams of children flow,
And forth the agèd greybeards go;

And spurn the blossoms, meek and sweet,
Of spring that bloom beneath their feet,

And pass them with an eager mind,
Intent the Wonder-flower to find.

Some homeward wander, dazed and dark,
Some on the mountain-side lie stark;

But none of all from town or tower
E'er find the magic Wonder-flower.

BIRD AND BARD.

Unbosom thyself, O lark, on high,
Sing thy song to the morning sky :
Trill and thrill till the wide blue air
That seemed but light seems music too,—
A tremulous melody everywhere,
Sinking down like a sounding dew;
Thyself dissolved therein, and we
Lost in thy carolling losing thee.

Sing thy song, O poet, on high,
Fuse thyself with the morning sky,
So the light of life shall flow more fair
That it thrilleth and filleth with song from thee—
Thy music a presence everywhere—
Thyself dissolved therein, that we,
Heedless of thee, may love thy lays,
And praise thee when God alone we praise.

HIC JACET.

How strange it seems with silent breath to stand
    within the place of death,
While earth and every living thing awaken to the
    breeze of spring,—
A gentle breeze that scarce upheaves the lime's light
    robe of early leaves.

In any form will any day restore to us the pass'd
    away?
Will any future new Love rise from out the sod where
    dead Love lies,
As this year's roses bud and blow o'er last year's
    blooms in mould below?

He was so bright he seemed to be a creature of
    eternity,
But now he lieth there as cold as any corpse of
    wormy mould;
No resurrection shall be known—no angel roll away
    the stone.

Cast solemnly the clods of clay upon him ere we turn
    away,
And stand in rev'rent silence by, and let no tear
    bedim the eye,
Nor any more lament be said than this lament—that
    Love is dead.

A MEDITATION.

Shall, in that state where good is crown'd with best,
    And perfect life fulfils life's prophecy,
This form terrene with many a pleasaunce blest,
    Be as a robe disused and put by ?

Or shall some climax thereunto belong,—
    Some counterpart in that th' immortal gains
To this melodious burst of matin song,—
    This mist of morning sunlight in the lanes ?

And shall it bring the knowledge what did mean
 The blueness of these heavens; and wherefore
  meant
This valley with its sloping swards of green,
 That fill the silent spirit with content?

Enough, if but the new take up the old,
 Transfigured though it be by that fresh birth;
And lift from grief to glory I behold
 The sweet familiar beauties of the earth.

Enough, if I be not as one that fears
 Strange forms, new tongues; but more as one, in
  truth,
Who knows his exile ended, that he hears
 The unforgotten music of his youth.

THE WISHING-BRIDGE.

The old bridge from the city grey
   Lieth no further than a mile,
   O'er many a rude sequester'd stile
And many a daisied meadow way;

And 'twixt green banks with wild blooms bright,
   And copses where the song-bird calls,
   The rivulet flows in silver falls,
And laughing ripples warm with light.

Come here in simple trust, O you
   Whose trust no cold experience shakes—
   Who have the fervent faith that makes
A truth of that it would have true!

Come when the sun that soon must set,
    Lingers in love about the place,
    And earth is as an angel's face
O'ershadow'd by a vague regret :

And when the dizzy insect hum
    Is hush'd in reverence to the power
    And solemn beauty of the hour
That makes the woods and valleys dumb.

Then, baptized by the setting sun
    In liquid hues of dying day,
    Unself thyself till thou canst pray
That the diviner will be done.

LYRICS OF LOVE AND DEATH,

ETC.

OLAF'S GUESTS.

Jarl Olaf he summon'd his henchmen all
And bade them make ready his banquet-hall;

" This night my sires of the dead," said he,
" Will come from Walhalla to sup with me."

So they set on the board the feast-lights dim,
And the mead-cups fill'd with mead to the brim;

And oped on the darkness the broad hall-door,
That the guests of the grave to the feast might pour.

Through the pine-wood went a shimmering light,
And the ban-dog bay'd to the moonless night.

In they filed—one by one—with noiseless tread,
Till the hall was throng'd with the shapes of the dead:

Each stood to the board with his vizor up—
Each lift to his lips the mead-brimm'd cup—

Each spake as he stood Jarl Olaf's name—
Each beckon'd unto him, then went as they came.

Jarl Olaf he rose in his harness dight
And follow'd them forth into the night;—

And the darkness closed on their ghostly track,
And never again came Olaf back.

JARL HALDOR'S DAUGHTER.

By the wayside stood holy Erik,
And lifted his voice and cried—
"Turn, O ye sons of the Norseman,
To Jesus the Crucified!"

"Stranger, and what is thy Saga,
And what new song do we hear?
Good are the songs of our fathers,
And pleasant unto the ear;"

Answer'd the grey Jarl Haldor;
"And many brave runes I ken—
Loving to gather round me,
Singers and Sagamen."

Then to him turn'd holy Erik,
And told him in measure good
The story of Mary Mother,
And of Christ who died on rood;

But out spake grey Jarl Haldor,
"Let him to the new Gods kneel
Who loveth his mother's distaff
More than his father's steel.

"Why have I sought rejoicing,
The rolling storm-wave o'er,
The song of the sword and buckler,
And the fray on the foeman's shore?

"And what shall avail the sunlight,
Or the sea-lift's laughing spray,
If the men of many battles
And the old Gods pass away?

"Let *me* be led hereafter,
When in fierce fight I fall,
By the wild-haired Valkyr maidens
To Father Odin's hall!

"To Walhall, hall of heroes,
Wherein I hope indeed
To eat of the wild boar Seimnerr,
And to drink of the beer and mead;

"And with mighty men of valour
To wage perpetual war,
And to look on Father Odin,
And the true old Hammerer, Thor."

But the daughter of Jarl Haldor
To the good man nearer drew,
And a mist of tears enshrouded
Her eyes of living blue.

And she said, " O Father Haldor
To this new faith give ear,
Which to valour addeth pity,
And with love doth conquer fear;

" And to the warrior giveth
A warfare all his days,
Yet leads his feet to triumph
By newer, nobler ways."

Then answer'd grey Jarl Haldor :—
" They are dead, the glorious throng
Who loved the Norseman's battle
And the joy of spear and song ;

" And now the new day bringeth
New feelings, fashions strange,
And the old is borne before us
On the rushing wind of change;

" Yet since the maid thou movest
(Wiser are maids than men),
I would hear thee, O strange singer,
Of this thy song again."

DEAD MINNA.

As May's first morn arose in pride,
The village maiden, Minna, died.

Her friends—the kinsmen of her race—
Mourn'd round her for a little space,

Then left her in her death-robe drest,
With one white lily on her breast.

But when the hour of night was near,
And moonlight soft suffused the bier,

There came the Prince of all the land,
And, weeping, kiss'd her small cold hand;

And brought a jewell'd circlet rare
To glimmer round the maiden's hair,

And brought a pearl-lit star to rest
Upon the crownèd maiden's breast.

Still bore her brow the moon's soft ray—
It tinged the lily where it lay.

He cast the circled gems aside—
" God's crown is best, my queen, my bride ! "

He cast the pearls beneath his feet—
" God's lily is thy breast-flow'r, Sweet ! "

Then, kneeling, wept with passionate pain,
And shower'd wild kisses down like rain;

And linger'd till the moon sank low,
And all its soft and smiling glow

Paled slowly from the pallid face,
And darkness rose around the place—

Then left her in her death-robe drest,
With one white lily on her breast.

EDWIN TO ANGELINA.

If one could cover vain love as they cover a dead
   man's face,
Cover and close for ever, and bury it out of
   sight,
Nor start at its hollow ghost haunting each silent
   place,
Vexing the dreary hours of the dim monotonous
   night;—

If one could learn at last the lore of the fluent smile and lie,—
Could batten with gross content upon life's material good,
And know no more of love than the name, at need to apply
To clothe convenience sordid in love's similitude;—

If one, indeed, as swine in the slough of sloth and of sin
Could wallow, and wish no other, and always thus could be,
Secure from the devils of memory ever entering in
And goading him forth from his garbage to drown in the sea;—

Or could one in barter take for youth and its glorious
 spoils,
Its fervour, its fiery passion, its nobler faith and
 doubt,
His indifference wise whom the world hath ta'en in
 its toils,
And bound down his breast to the grindstone and
 ground his heart out ;—

If on some lonely height of frigid, intellectual
 morn,
The sov'reign mind the heart could savagely tame
 and rule ;
And deaden its burning nerve in a Lethe of lasting
 scorn,
As hot iron is thrust into water to hiss itself
 cool ;—

Better a Patriot's death—straight from the street to the sod,

In the dim and misty day-break forth for some good cause led,

To look one's last undaunted—the while a marching squad

Halted, front-faced, loaded, and suddenly shot one dead!

For when I strive to make such feast as the evil Fates afford,

And gather such guests as gather to misery's holiday—

In glides the ghost, and shadowy sits at the board,

Poisons the few poor meats and scares the feasters away.

So have the Destinies will'd it! Ever may life mean
    joy to you,
That means to me but patience—that virtue of snails
    and slaves;—
May you find new loves as fair as the old was
    only true—
But would to God that ghosts could keep at home in
    their graves!

THE LOVER'S MESSAGE.

[TEMP. CAR. II.]

Go, Bird of Eve, and warble clear
This message in my mistress' ear;—
Tell her that love is sweet, O sweet,
When lover and his lady meet,
And she with smiles and tender wiles
His longing gaze doth greet, doth greet!

And this too tell her, sweet, O sweet!—
That youthful hours so fast do fleet,
That love whose suit is long delay'd,
And coldly met when warmly made,
Must seek a nest in some new breast
Before the flow'rs do fade, do fade.

Yet whisper softly, sweet, O sweet !—
That knight ne'er knelt at lady's feet
Who did so fondly, wildly sue,
So loth to change old loves for new ;
And if she's kind, she none shall find
In all the world so true, so true !

BARNEWOOD BELLS.

When we two wander'd forth first together,
Wander'd together the breezy dells,
The spring smiled out with sudden flushes,
And I read your thought in your tender blushes—
" Gloria Deo ! " rang Barnewood Bells ;
" Gloria Deo ! Gloria Deo !
" Gloria Deo ! " rang Barnewood Bells.

The air was faint with the summer blisses,
And full of the soft, sonorous swells—
As again in the pause of our happy kisses,
Too happy, sweet, for a life like this is—
   Gloria Deo ! " rang Barnewood Bells ;
" Gloria Deo ! Gloria Deo !
" Gloria Deo ! " rang Barnewood Bells.

The autumn leaves lay sere by the river,
When false tongues drave us to cold farewells—
The evil angels were strong to sever,
And the morning of life was lost for ever;—
" Gloria Deo ! " rang Barnewood Bells,
" Gloria Deo ! Gloria Deo !
Gloria Deo ! " rang Barnewood Bells.

Now as I thrust, with too idle weeping,
The frozen grass from the stone that tells
Where thou liest, more blest than living,
Faithful to death, and in death forgiving;—
" Gloria Deo ! " ring Barnewood Bells,
" Gloria Deo ! Gloria Deo !
Gloria Deo ! " ring Barnewood Bells.

DORA HERBERT.

SWEET Dora Herbert, flow'ret nurst
By nature, fed with sun and shower,
Till like an Eden-blossom burst
The right bud into brighter flower;
She seem'd by angels brought to earth,
From some remote and happy star,
Or claiming for her place of birth
A clime of summers fairer far.

I loved to mark her life's young spring,
From day to day, from week to week;
Each birth of morning seem'd to bring
A richer bloom upon her cheek;
Her eyes of tender hazel, O!
To watch them was a dear delight,
Now moist with tears they loved to glow,
Now crowded full of soulborn light.

What note, where birds of Eastern wing
Bright-plumaged to the rose rejoice,
Or falling waters in the spring
Had half the music of her voice?—
Now light with laughter, now with speed,
To sweet and solemn changed from gay.
At some old tale of knightly deed,
Or some high-thoughted poet's lay.

Most vain is love, hard sages preach,
When we the wish'd-for guerdon wear,
But what is love when love must teach
The lesson of its own despair?
So every thought that robed with state,
That crown'd her brow with light divine,
But served to show the space more great
'Twixt her and any hope of mine.

In vain I strove my thought to turn
From that false dream of joy and pain,
Departed, passion to unlearn,
Return'd, to learn it all again;
Till, wearied in my soul, I swore
It ill became a man to shun
His fate, so ere the day was o'er,
Sweet Dora should be lost or won.

That hour the birds of air were glad,

Their summer store of song and glee

Was all unspent, the roses had

Bright noons of beauty yet to be;

And, richer far, myself 'twas plain

Had love to last the longest life,

And lives beyond it could I gain

Sweet Dora Herbert for my wife.

Below her garden's terraced crest,

All urns and palisades, lay hid

A leafy glen, her wonted rest,

Through which a singing streamlet slid;

As onward through the murm'rous shade,

She moved in stateliness and grace,

I deem'd her queen of glen and glade,

The young Egeria of the place.

From lawn and garden came the breeze,
Scent laden through the umbrage blew,
Made music mid the murmuring trees,
And from the violet shook the dew,
Then ceased. The song that now it sings
Is not that song of Love's young breath,
But fair from unforgotten springs
Bloom roses mid the weeds of death.

THREE KISSES.

Three kisses I give each morning to Willie, so lithe and bright,
And three to merry Elsie, with her dancing curls of light,
And three I give no longer that I gave in days of old,
To lips that were ever ready, but now are for ever cold:

But when Willie has hush'd his ranting in awe of the dark without,
And Elsie lingers in silence our household knees about,
There comes a small voice pleading through the sound of wind and rain,
And a small wraith through the darkness flits by the window pane;

So when each lies softly folded and with happy slumber blest,
And the dreams that visit children come floating round their rest,
I follow the wind o'er the moorland away to the churchyard lone,
And leave there tears for kisses on my little maid's grave-stone.

IDA'S GIFT.

WHITE rosebuds Ida gave me,
And your gift as soon forgot,
If to mock me or enslave me
Matters not;
Dead, and I now to die,
'Twere meet that dust with dust should lie.

Perchance that when my bosom
With life shall beat anew,
I may find you fair in blossom,
Quicken'd too,
See you wake, rise and take
And seek out Eden for your sake :—

There I, for you appealing,
Will say, "Not these condemn,
All my best of thought and feeling
Gave I them;"
Yield you so, rise and go
Unto the unblest shades below.

Then the thought indeed shall brave me,
However lost, undone,
That of any gifts she gave me
Lost I none:
Taintless, pure, each her wooer,
As he received did give back to her.

THE LAUREL CROWN.

When in the strife of life, love's chaplet falls from the head,
And the roses in pleasure's garland are drooping and dead,
Where shall the crownless look to win him a crown instead?

Though the wreath remain that is wove of the leaf the lightning spares,
Which he at the battle's close who hath fought a good fight wears,
His guerdon who greatly suffers, his glory who greatly dares;—

How shall he seek to win it—by smiting some sin anew?

By setting his heel on the false and setting on high the true?

By oping the city gates that the armies of God march through?

If for such seeming service the wreath of glory were meet,

How should I wear it in triumph who wavered so oft in defeat,

While the saints who are strong before Thee cast all their crowns at Thy feet!

Rather let all world-voices shout with a trumpet blast,

"This man failed and was vanquish'd," so that Thou hold me fast,

And crownless, I find my crown low at Thy feet at last.

A SHOOTING STAR, OBSERVED FROM THE SEA.

LIKE a love-stricken maiden, sad and young,
Mad, helpless, heedless, down a swift stream borne
To death 'mid the twined water-weeds forlorn,
Leaving her passionate wrongs unwept, unsung,
With none to heed her on her wild death way,
And none to bend above her bier and say,
" God pity her, she died young!"

So wentest thou, pale daughter of the night,
Borne swiftly down th' immeasurable blue,
Then sank beneath its liquid depths from view;
Meanwhile thy myriad sisters shone as bright,
But our hearts turnèd from them where they shone,
To thee, the beautiful, the past and gone,
And mourn'd thy vanish'd light.

We sat and mused by the dirge-murm'ring sea,
How loveliest things have ever briefest breath,
How beauty is the stolen spouse of death,
And hearts are reft of hopes as heaven of thee ;
And each one thought of some fair star, that went
In silence from his life's lorn firmament,
No more again to be.

And as the seaman from his bark, storm-riven,
Casts forth her argosied wealth into the main,
Did each one put away from him with pain
And silence many a hope that youth had given ;
So died they in thy death. Their funeral song
Was borne the desolate dashing waves along,
Beneath the darken'd heaven.

THE FINAL BLOW.

I MARVELL'D not at speech or smile
    Withheld, or to some better given;
Through sloughs of trial one stumbles, while
    Another treads the seventh heaven.

So far you deem'd my deeds of good,
    My knowledge of the good below;
In such weak mood was ill withstood—
    I own'd to all the angels so.

So when you met my vows with slight,
    I could not chide the wise mistrust,
But judged you right in heart's despite,
    And thought you tender, knew you just.

One worships where he may not win,
    And far the bitterer pang did prove,
Ah! not wherein you scorn'd my sin,
    But that you scorn'd me in my love.

For while you thought of that as true,
    My altar held one sacred spark;
Quench or renew? 'twas left to you,
    Cold stands the altar in the dark!

IN THE SPRING.

See, there is greenness, fresh greenness all over the
 wood,
 And the primrose is proud of her crown of gold;
God is surely tender and good,
 Though the world be weary and old.

The early orchis burns, like sun-touch'd wine, in the
 wood,
 The dove hath blisses half dream'd, half told;
God is surely tender and good,
 Though the world be weary and old.

My father cursed, my mother turn'd away,
    Her blessing to my piteous pray'r denied,
Yet seem'd the very voice of Heav'n to say,
    "Bear all, and be his bride."

He whose least word seem'd beautiful and right,
    Soon as to wifely cares my bliss was wean'd,
Grew foul with shameful riot in my sight,
    And falser than the fiend.

Some women would have far more briefly wept,
    But, nursing all their spirit for the deed,
Had given him the dagger while he slept,
    Though damn'd, avenged and freed.

But then his babe upon my lap was laid,
    To keep me pure from sinning. In the boy
To see his father's smile ere it betray'd,
    Was something of a joy.

Yet this they would not leave me. When spring sods
    Shook off their winter sadness for fresh bloom,
They piled up to the very sky the clods
    That press'd him in the tomb.

But when the poplar's shadow slowly sways
    Across the moon-lit wall, on many a night
The lost one steals unto my breast, and stays
    And clasps me tight, so tight;

And though he wears each curl he used to wear,
    And his cheek dimples as it did in dreams,
Of this my solace none of them will hear,
    And I am mad, it seems.

See, there is greenness, fresh greenness, all over the
    wood,
    And the primrose is proud of her crown of gold;
God is surely tender and good,
    Though the world be weary and old.

THE WAYSIDE SHRINE.

'Twas up a Valais mountain-road
   To gain the pass my feet did press,
While far aloft the snow-peaks show'd
   In awful aching loneliness;
O'er half way clouds ascending high,
Like second mountains in the sky.

Grey boulders strew'd the rugged path,
   That from the bolt-scarr'd heights seemed hurl'd
By demons, striving in their wrath
   To work the ruin of the world;
The glacier-torrents wrought a roar
Of many waters evermore.

All else was wildly strange, for steep
  And high the pine-girt pastures rose,
Up which the nimble goat would leap
  Unto the limit of the snows;
Or where broke through the rock's rent walls
A silvery mist of waterfalls.

'Mid crag and gorge o'ergloom'd with shade
  A chalet gleam'd; a pleasant sound
The goat-bell's fitful tinkle made,
  And the blue gentian bloom'd around;
The path, by whomsoever trod,
'Twere meet he paused there to praise God.

Soon, at a turning of the way,
  I came across a road-side shrine,
So placed that he who could not pray
  Might gain from Nature aid divine—

There her best wealth she did accord
Unto the altar of the Lord.

Rude was the shrine—a stone wherein
    An image of the mother-maid
Was set, uncouth, ill shaped, and in
    Coarse tawdry ornament array'd ;
Strange were it could a form so mean
Raise any soul to the Unseen.

In presence of the mountain's face,
    Where heaven makes light of human years,
A passer by might deem the place
    Disfigured by such lowly cares ;
A higher art, with unshod feet,
Would halt where God and Nature meet.

Yet there a poor herdwoman knelt
    Absorb'd, and heedless of my view,

Despite her tears drew strength, and felt
    Communion with the pure and true ;
Then rose, and climb'd with lighter air,
And freer for that wayside prayer.

I watch'd her less'ning form toil slow
    To the lone chalet on the height,
And knew that talk with angels so
    Leaves round the earthly body light;
That whatsoe'er the shrine appear,
'Twas good for her to have been here.

Ne'er dawn'd on her perception dim
    The virgins Raphael portray'd
From faces heav'n sent forth to him,
    San Sisto's or Foligno's maid,
Nor Milan's marbles, nor the dome
Wherewith great Angelo crown'd Rome.

The spirit that no form contains,
  The abstract from all concrete free,
The heav'n that earthly shape disdains
  Had never won the bended knee,
She did to this mean shape award
Of the sweet mother of the Lord.

No thund'rous avalanche astir
  To rush the startled vales upon,
Nor glint of steel-blue glacier
  That like an angel's armour shone,
Had awed her thus, nor sun that rose
To glorify the morning snows.

The highest humanness allied
  To hers she sought at that low shrine,
Unable from the spirit's side
  T' approach at once to the divine

Nor find a comfort or a charm
In disembodying faith from form.

Does he who parts from form because
    It sinks, not serves, his spirit's needs,
Or deems he holds in some large laws
    The quintessence of all the creeds,
Find his cold mountain airs too rare
For breath of rev'rence or of prayer?

Does he despise their insight dim,
    These simple ones, their rites condemn,
Because heav'n soars so high for him,
    That seems to stoop so low to them—
Yet leaves to them to tend the creed,
To fruit of duty and good deed?

The truth they serve but cannot see,
    Sees he yet serves not—does he say

"The things they guess are clear to me"—
    Yet fail to follow and obey?
And work the soul less service thence,
    Than they who serve it through the sense?

And is he fain to feed his pride
    Where their humilities are fed,
Forgetting that the deified
    Dispenses all their daily bread
Of food celestial, though the store
Be an irregular less or more?

Let him, descending hither, kneel,
    And e'en through this poor form adore,
And with a contrite spirit feel
    That God is nearer than before—
And own, whate'er the shrine appear,
'Tis good for him to have been here.

JEZER HORRA.

So the children of the Captivity
Lift up their voices with one accord,
Because that their hands from bondage free
Had built again the house of the Lord;
With trumpet, and cymbal, and joyful roar,
The Priests and Levites and people stood,
Praising the Lord, for the Lord is good,
Whose mercy endureth evermore.

But the ancient men and the elders, they
Who had seen great Solomon's house of old,
Rememb'ring all that had pass'd away,
The Ark and the Cherubim of gold,
The Mercy seat, the Shekinah cloud,
The Urim and Thummim of days gone by,
Cried out with a great and bitter cry,
Rended their raiment and wept aloud.

Then Zacharias the prophet spake,
"Full well do ye weep and wail, for ye
Did the law of the Lord your God forsake
Till he drave you into captivity;
And though his mercies return, yet none
Renounceth the sin of his sires of old,
For there moveth among you, uncontroll'd,
Jezer Horra, that evil one!"

Then all the people shouted, " To-day
Show us this Prince of the evil Pow'rs,
Him will we take, and bind, and slay,
That the sin of our fathers be not ours;
Lest we too feel the avenging rod,
And the temple again be burn'd with fire,
Because we follow our heart's desire,
Leaving the law of the Lord our God."

But Zacharias answer'd them, " Lo!
Him can ye nowise take and slay,
For the Lord commandeth that to and fro
About the earth he shall walk alway:
This may ye do, with a constant mind
Daily and hourly resist his pow'r,
Jealously keeping each day and hour
The Holy Law in your hearts enshrined."

And while they clamour'd aloud, behold!
The gates of the Temple open swung,
And a terrible lion, fierce and bold,
Forth from the yawning portal sprung;
Strong and swart and angry and dun,
The breath of his nostrils like fire was red,
"This is none other," the people said,
"Than Jezer Horra, the evil one."

"Fear not, but bind him with chains full strong,
The Lord our helper shall with us fight,
And the powers of evil shall know ere long
The name Jehovah is Judah's might."
And when they had bound him strong and fast,
The host of the people that stood without,
Rejoiced with a great and joyful shout,
"Jezer Horra is chain'd at last!"

But they fell on their faces sore afraid,

As the captive was taken away from sight,

And forth whence his broken bonds were laid,

One like to an angel, piercing bright,

Ascended slowly the morning sky,

With raiment that shone as the morning sun,

And face as the face of a Holy One,

Unto the throne of the Most High.

Then Zacharias the prophet said,

" This shall be unto you for a sign;

The evil one is a lion dread

To rend and tear you when ye incline

To follow your idols and lusts abhorr'd;

But when ye resist, and strive, and shun,

Then Jezer Horra, the evil one,

Is a sun-bright angel of the Lord."

POEMS OF DISILLUSION.

THE AMPHITHEATRE.

THE folk of a city old and grey,
To the amphitheatre flock'd one day,
For the gods themselves had announced a play
Of the many boons, without which, they say,
Man's life were nought in its transient stay,
    But a little dust.

First did the arrowy young god rise,
Cupid, the darts of his dangerous eyes
Are shafts full sharp, and in ev'ry wise
They wound men's hearts that they bleed in sighs,
Till at last, through lust or change, Love dies
    To a little dust.

Then Jove-born Bacchus leapt, bright and strong,
Into the midst of the laughing throng,
With his winy bowl and his fiery song,
Follow'd with pomp of cymbal and gong;
But dull satiety sank ere long
  To a little dust.

Then suddenly started Mars, the red,
With shielded arm and helmeted head;
Terror and Flight were his horses dread;
Songs and shouts in his praise were said,
Till the shouters saw when the fight was dead
  But a little dust.

Then in came Plutus, the lame and blind,
Who scattereth wealth with uncertain mind;
Of all that seek there be few that find,
And his gifts are ever of wingèd kind;
And suddenly fleeing leave behind
  But a little dust.

And many more shows were shown, they say;
But if you would seek the place to-day
Among the wrecks of the pass'd away
Of that amphitheatre old and grey,
There is nought of it or its crowd so gay
    But a little dust.

DISILLUSION.

They are clearing the anchor-cable,
    The mariners crowd to the fore,
And over the bar of the harbour
    We glide to the olden shore.

And the sunlight falls on the castle,
    The slow moving sails of the mill,
The white and ancient lighthouse
    And the kirk on the wind-swept hill;

And gilds with a tenderer glory
  The graves where the seamen sleep ;
Content that their burial silence
  Be stirr'd by the voice of the deep.

The swell of the soothed summer ocean
  Dissolves into silvery spray,
And lifts with a languid motion
  The pilot-boat out in the bay.

Ah, fair ! yet the first days and fairest,
  That, yielding their beauty and breath,
Were led by the angel of slumber
  To the arms of the angel of death !

But could we their far-off Hades
  Fling open and bid them arise,
With the light and the ancient passion
  Relit in their strange dead eyes,

Their light would reveal such darkness,
    Their pleasure recall such pain,
That 'twere better, silently, softly,
    To lay them to rest again.

Yet fall, O thou earlier splendour,
    On shore and on basking bay
One moment!—" Wake up, man, we're landing!
    Beware of the cheats on the quay!"

AFTER-DINNER TALK.

Your story is neither good nor new,
  The manner fine, nor the moral fair,
But the bottle has tarried its time with you,
  Send it this way for change of air.
True, as you say, his life elysian,
  Our friend now finds turn'd inside out;
He sees all things with an alter'd vision,
  And is astonished thereat, no doubt.

Poor fellow ! so hot, so enthusiastic
   For "freedom," "enlightenment," " rights of man,"
" Progress," " philanthropy," moulding the plastic
   Child Nature on some new ideal plan ;
His " mission," too—ah ! that was a gay word,
   Just fitted the castle of cards to crown ;—
But a little whiff from a lady wayward
   Has tumbled, you see, the card-house down.

That one who has donn'd the virile dress,
   And rasps each day at a rugged chin,
Should the wreck of a whole life's aims confess,
   When two blue eyes he has fail'd to win !
I've earn'd my scars in the fight too, Maurice,
   Yet sit a hale bachelor here, you see ;
And they'll now as soon flirt with an Ichthyosaurus
   As think of setting their caps at me.

I have known, as I say, the madness too—
  A lunacy brief, although intense;
Some notes and a wither'd flow'r or two
  Testify here against common sense:
Odd does it seem, to see them laid
  'Mid these mouldy books with their dusty backs—
These, the "Statistics of Foreign Trade,"
  And this "The Law upon Income Tax."

What leaps of the happy heart when she came!
  What sudden transitions from dark to bright!
What pacings beneath her window-frame
  At unwonted hours of morn and night!
Perhaps for other ends I was made,
  With other aims I have long since striven;
Think you they'll rub off the rust of trade,
  And make us lovers again in Heaven?

Fools that we are, we must needs be blest,
    When we give a woman our brains in fee,
And carve with the blade of youthful zest
    Our Rosalind's name on every tree.
Faugh! the fancy was once divine,
    Now it is gross and dark and cold;
Fill up your glass, there is nought like wine
    When the world and the heart are growing old.

'Tis nature, say, to be vex'd therewith,
    And to waste thereon some idle groans;
When we find that the honest heart of Smith
    Counts nothing against the gold of Jones;
No matter! If old wounds bleed afresh,
    What styptic is like the lust of gain?
Let your mournful friend, if he will, lose flesh,
    He trades in sorrow, and I with Spain.

I don't go mending the world's condition
    Till my own condition is parish-food,
Nor own to having another "mission"
    Than the mission to keep my digestion good.
I deem Dame Knowledge a savage ogress,
    Who swallows her children a score per minute,
And fancy the "March of Human Progress"
    Has one or two bars of the "Rogue's March" in it.

In spite of the saints and sages, I
    Am wisely and well content, forsooth,
To let the philanthropies blow by,
    And the noisy passions that pass for truth;
And I hold that life were a simple song
    Were the blacks all black and the whites all white,
Nor so much of right in this man's wrong,
    Nor so much of wrong in that man's right.

Till the end of life's dizzy whirl shall come,
    Let us strive as we can to keep sound skins ;
Our earth is a clumsy teetotum
    That reels and buzzes, and kicks and spins ;
And men and women, from peer to peasant,
    Are tools or tyrants as fate's chance brings ;
And who shall say which is most pleasant
    To be the puppet or pull the strings ?

Your rainbow-robe of idealness
    May be flaunting wear for upper ether,
But I hold my dull, grey homespun dress
    Best for terrestrial wind and weather :
And he is the wisest man, I ween,
    Who to narrowest knowledge makes pretence,
And lights on the balancing point between
    The opposite poles of soul and sense.

One man with truth in his farthest ken,
   Follows with ardour her troublous track,
Flounders about for a while and then
   Cannot go forward or turn back.
Another, no perilous path seeks he,
   But the senses sway at his swinish feast;
Watch them a little, and what do you see?
   One is a dreamer, and one a beast.

My fancy to no extreme inclines,
   That which is evil is that which is odd,
So I love to kneel at the well-worn shrines,
   And to worship well-to-do people's God;
To tune the pew from the parson's perch
   I take to my soul as wisdom plain;
But when I am safely home from church,
   Say " *Que sais je?*" with old Montaigne.

All high-flown fancies of love and life
    Are soon puff'd out by experience sad,
For first the world, and next your wife,
    You find are false, then yourself as bad ;
In morals too, he can best afford
    To shun the fight who shrinks the fall—
When my virtues take their turn at the board
    Two moves from the devil checkmates them all.

Then lay romance, my boy, on the shelf,
    Though the world or the women should use you ill,
Though Daphne prefer a peer to yourself,
    Or Chloe marry a cotton-mill.
Here is my pamphlet, wet from the press,
    You need not read it, so don't look askance ;
And, come what may, we will none the less
    Find solace in this good wine of France.

THE DEVIL AND DOCTOR FAUSTUS.

SAID the Devil to Doctor Faustus,
 "I have watch'd thee for years a score,
And to see a fine man buried
 Grieveth my heart full sore.

"Thine eyes are dim for a lover's,
 Through peering in vain for truth;
Yet thy lips are athirst for kisses,
 As the yearning lips of youth.

" Thy brow is wrinkled with study,
 But thou hast not gain'd in the school
What brings the maid in her beauty
 Unto the breast of the fool.

" Thou art great in lore and science,
 But thou hast made all thy ways
The ways of lonely virtue,
 And not of pudding or praise.

" So the world speaks lightly of thee,
 Seeing thee blink in thy den—
' This musty, fusty scholar,
 Is as an owl 'mong men.'

" Thou losest the joy of nature,
 The zest of the social game ;
Pleasure and pow'r thou foregoest,
 And the sweet incense of fame.

"Now, therefore, I promise unto thee
  Thy vanish'd youth to restore,
And to make thee fresher and fairer
  Than ever thou wert before;

" I will smooth thy brow of its wrinkles,
  And send thee forth richly array'd,
And make thee the gayest gallant
  That ever befool'd a maid.

" Each day shall give some new pleasure,
  Each night shall bring some new bliss,
And thy lips, that so long were lonely,
  Shall thrill with the warmth of a kiss.

" I will put thy wisdom to profit,
  Till all men shall worship and say—
'Lo! this is the great Herr Faustus,
  The foremost man of the day!'

"I will give thee pow'r o'er nature,
Nor the sway of mankind deny,
And the little matter of payment
We can think of by and by."

Then answer'd Faustus, "O Satan,
Thou readest my heart like a scroll,
And thy voice, that has spoken to me,
Is as the voice of my soul;

"Why slave for an unknown future,
With weary bosom and brow,
And what shall avail the hereafter,
When one has lost the now?

"This life is the one thing certain,
Wherefore the bargain let's try;
And the little matter of payment
We will talk of by and by."

THE JESTER'S SONG.

There's nought in this world, for king or for clown,
But a kiss when you're up, and a kick when you're down;
Feathers or rags,
So the world wags!

There's nought in this world but to starve or to cheat,
And the fool's the knave's jackal to find him in meat;
Bare legs or hose,
So the world goes.

There's nought in this world, when you're in it no more,
But to lie in your grave with a lie graven o'er;
Foemen or friends,
So the world ends!

POEMS IN BLANK VERSE.

SIR LANCELOT AT THE CROSS.

AND so it fell that he, Sir Lancelot, rode
All day across a waste and wither'd land,
Wherein was voice of nothing, and none dwelt;
And with the set of sun a country came
Wherein none dwelt, but many castles lay
Rent, ruinous, irregular with the fall
Of carvings and of columns—silent save
With creeping murmur moved the worm decay
Where life and pleasure erst o'er cup and kiss
Each other hail'd immortal. Forth he fared,

Mute and much marvelling, while many a league,
The yew that nurseth shadows in her shape
Held sway, and any winds that wander'd through
Were as lost souls, that call'd on some to save,
Mock'd with a mighty silence for reply.
Then sought Sir Lancelot comfort of a pray'r—
And thus he spake—" O fair sweet Lord, I pray
Me sick that thou make sound, me foul make pure
And holy, gazing on the holy Grail!"

And while the stars were gathering, forth he came
Unto a desert place where two ways met—
A desert and strange place, and hard by saw
A cross of marble carven curiously,
With shapes of saints and virgins stoled in stone;
There Lancelot loosed his helm, and laid him down,
And was as one that dreameth him a dream.

And, as one seeth in dreams, he saw a knight

On litter by two fair white palfreys borne,

Brought wounded to the cross. His vizor lift,

Show'd the wan life that linger'd in his cheek,

O'erlaid by leaden death. His helpless weight

Sank heavily, his harness smote the stone

With clangour, and he pray'd—" O fair, sweet Lord,

Because I, even though I fall, yet fall

Face forward, fighting through the fiends to Thee,

Nor turn for dalliance or delight aside,

For this my travail yield me of Thy grace,

I may be holpen of the holy Grail!"

And even while he spake was straightway brought

The sacred vessel of the Sangreal, laid

Upon pure silver; round it tapers four,

Set in fair silver, seeming borne by none,

Save an uncertain mystery of wings,

Soon lost in light intense. The wounded knight,

Kneeling with difficult patience, kiss'd the cup,
And, lo! his ghostly pallor changed to rose,
And with a sudden smile he took his youth
In all his veins at once, and stood erect,
In all the points of knighthood such a knight
As in the tumult of the tournament
Lays his lance gaily for a lady's grace.

Then fell it that Sir Lancelot would arise
To touch for his soul's health the Sangreal blest,
But vainly. Seeking, the desire to seek
Wax'd weak for visions rising in the way,
Of how in lilied bowers of Camelot
He lay, the guilty guest of Queen Ganore.

Again he strove—again, and yet again;
But, thrall'd and troubled with tumultuous joy
His thoughts came thick, as when a hand of chance
Touches a tone upon the string that brings

The past in passion to us. So the past,
Rich with remembrance of the luring lip—
The lip, the languorous heaving happy breast,
The deep delicious light of drowning eyes,
That down to desperate worship drew and drew—
Grew richer with remember'd treasons sweet,
But chief that first, when all the air was fill'd
With fatal music, and the fading light
That wanly shone o'er western skies and seas
Was blent of passion's blush and passion's pale,
And the wild want that took the heart of earth,
Desiring unto death the beautiful,
Came to them, sitting side by side, as each
Upon the tremulous silence sobb'd to each
The long-pent secret, until each for each
Cast heav'n aside, and with fierce blood-beats slew
The cold-voiced conscience. So the tide of love,
Beneath the moon of memory, rose in flood

O'er life, and all the records it had writ.

But when the vision pass'd he pray'd anew,

Much mourning. For the silvern show had ceased—

A solemn train of sailing angels bore

The service of the Sangreal to the stars—

And mute before bare heav'n he stood dismay'd,

As one shall stand before the judgment dumb,

Till from the void of stars there woke a voice,

Clear, awful, unappeasable, that seem'd

The conscience of the silence gathering speech,

That spake him—"Lancelot, wary as the wolf,

Swift as the libbard, as the lion strong,

Stern of thy sword and subtle of thy tongue,

And sinful, staining all thy soul with sin,

Sweet, secret; thee, by penance and slow pain,

Pray'r, fasting, vigils wearily bought and borne,

May God assoil! But never any more

Thou in the garden of thine innocence

Shalt walk as in the days when thou wert pure,

Nor canst thou kiss the Sangreal with the kiss

Of children or of angels ; wherefore hence

Arise, and hie thee from this holy place !"

Then rose Sir Lancelot, sorrowful, and strode

His quivering steed ; and 'neath a night, whose stars

Seem'd falling in a large and luminous rain,

Rode to salt shores, where many mighty waves

Smote the sea-marge with thunder, roar on roar.

PILATE IN EXILE.

ROMAN, whether of Cæsar's wrath thrust forth
From Tiber's shore, like bale be thine to mine,
Doom'd to the company of mountains cold,
Whose rifted crags writhe upward to the cloud;
Or whether I, long strange to men, a shade
See thee—a shade, scourged by th' avenging three,
Most dolorous, more accursed is he thou seest,
Pilate, erst governor of the Jews, ev'n he
Who slew the man of Galilee, the Christ!

For, day by day, there dawn th' eternal snows,
At rise or set smote by the angry sun,

Red with an awful trouble of just blood,—

In memory that I wrought the people's will,

The people's, when they all with one voice cried—

" Let him be crucified !"   And night by night,

Voiced with accusing wrath, the mighty winds

Hurl, mad with torture, on the pine-woods old,

That, bending, in their agony groan.   And forth

A far roar peals from echoing peak to peak,

Till the great snow-fall swalloweth the voice,

And hurrieth down to darkness.   For, behold !

When as I sat in judgment, him they brought

For judgment—this the King, whose unseen crown,

And worship wrested from the mocker's mouth,

And strength forlorn, and legion'd loneliness,

O'erlaid my power with power, and seem'd to wear

An armour that I wot not of.   Then rose

The rabble round me with their bribing breath,

And vile and vassal praise.   And, lo ! of me

That sought in years of youth that soul of things,
The Truth, by mystic Oracle 'twas told
That in the after-days the Truth should stand
Before me, lightly question'd, left to bear
Its slighted secret from me. This One spake
Of Truth,—then ask'd I wearily, " What is Truth ? "
Could one mouth be more wise than all the Schools ?
Could what Greece gave not come from Galilee ?
Are prisoners more than princes ? Should one seek
Philosophers in felons ? Then I spake,—
" Take him and crucify him"— whom they took
And slew, and Pilate yielded that they slew ;
Pilate, who saw no fault in him at all,
Yet slew the very Truth and Life, the Christ.

Th' unburied shades spurn'd from the Stygian boat,
Here move in mighty robes, whose misty folds
Veil the dim hills ; in vaporous crowd on crowd
They pass in haste, accusers of my soul !

For when they had set upon his cross the name
Of King, and crown'd with thorns and cool'd with gall,
At the ninth hour earth shook, the rocks were rent,
The land was dark, and many dead arose—
The sheeted dead strode straightway through the dark
Unto the palace where I, Pilate, lay,
And pointing lean and length'ning fingers, cried,
" Wo to thee, wo to thee ! what hast thou done ?
Thou that didst seek the Truth, didst slay the Truth ;
Hast slain the very Truth and Life, the Christ !"

Hence ! vex not with unsought companionship
The accursèd one.   Should fortune set thy feet
Romeward, bear witness thou hast Pilate seen ;
Whom not the wrath of Cæsar wreak'd with will
By the bleak elements, his ministers
Hath wrought this anguish ;—Pilate who sustains
Unslain the vengeance of a God, to whom
Rome hath no temple ;—Pilate, unto whom

Visions are given wherein the Shrines of Rome
Perish, the purples of the Cæsars pale,
The Capitoline Mount beholds no more
The coil of triumph toiling up its steep
With stately progress, serpentine and slow;—
Who sees the dust their fashion would defy
Heap'd upon halls imperial;—who sees
The statued Gods un-pedestall'd depart
Each after each, a doom upon their brows,
To darkness—while colossal fanes and fair
Climb to the clouds, and his their fame and praise
The lonely Galilean whom we slew!
Such knowledge brings the wand'ring night to me,
Pilate—to whom a curse of prophecy
Cleaves like a burning skirt—that murder made
And slew the very Truth and Life, the Christ.

THE NEW EVANGEL.

THE fool saith in his heart "There is no God."
Having first said therein "There is no good;"—
What if the wise man soar to the top of good
And find no God there? God being born of us,
Not we of him—our aggregate of good—
Growth of our thought and growing with our thought
From low to high, from many unto One—
And lifted on the level of our lives
As the flood lift the Ark to Ararat—
Created, not Creator—mutable—
The mould of His feign'd moulding moulding Him.

Such is the great new gospel—such the end
Of wisdom gain'd through ages. Time's first sons
Nought doubted, we the school'd of centuries
Nothing believe. Forthwith we crown man God,
The sciences his prophets, culture Christ,
The earth redeem'd by Physics his sole heav'n—
Supernal nought nor supernatural more—
Man, slave of death, shall yet be lord of life,
Himself unto himself both good and truth—
What more? The here is all, th' hereafter nought,
And the fond fancies that have gone before
To beautify the opposite shores of death
Have idly dream'd. The hopes that made themselves
Laws to the reason with their passionate will
Are vain, and vain the visions which the soul,
Like blindness prophesying of its sight,
Claims to have seen of that which it would see;
Vain too the soul itself—a self no more—

THE NEW EVANGEL.

A quintessence that moves from form to form,
First I, next thou, next one that is to be;
Doom'd like a bubble on the ocean's breast
To worship of the wave whereon 'tis borne,
Wherein it sinks its separate self again.

Earth! mother! thrice accursed because so fair,
Because so fond—shutting not life in life—
Letting thy children dream whom thou let'st die;
Sweet are thy summers, yet they stir us oft
With yearnings after summers otherwhere;
And sweet thy flowers, but straightway he who sees
Sickens for sight of far-off Asphodels,
And feigns of them as fadeless though these fade;
And sweet the loves thou bringest and we love—
But lo! the food hath made a hunger, lo!
For evermore the unappeasable heart
Seeketh, and finding is not satisfied,
But strives to snatch Love from thy doom of dust,

And with great greed of everlastingness
So dow'r him that thou could'st not rule with change
Nor cool with clay—but he were lord of thee
And laugher at thy limits. Sweet, too, death—
And sweet the sod thou givest us for graves,
Yet ever dost thou thwart desire to die
With anger at the nothingness of death;
And though thou steal the murmur from the mouth,
And draw the vision slowly from the eye,
And drop the lids on darkness—though thou lay
As slumber bids thee lay, the limbs—yet stays
A look unfinal on the face, a gaze
As of continuance, a haunting sense
Of something other worlds have won from ours—
So that we see not that the dead are dead.
Then, like a sudden laughter through the stars—
A splendid glory round the feet of God—
Comes the great thought of immortality!

And this, too, is but a fool's fantasy,
The mocking echo of a mad desire,
And soul and form are of one dust, and die—
So saith the prophet! On his page I slept
Full sadly, and full sadly dream'd a dream :—

I dream'd God perish'd, as a stricken sun,
From His mid-universe. His throne was void—
And lo! there rose before it, formless, vast,
Shadowy, impalpable, array'd with night—
That which reach'd forth a hand and laid the stars
To silence, that they ceased to murmur more
Their old processional song—nor sang nor shone,
But died with a dull glare as of white ash
Upon the cooling ember. Then my vision
Forsook the universal to behold
This earth alone : and I beheld it, night
Clothed on it like a vesture—light was not

And men were few, and each had to himself
A wilderness of shade. And each in soul
By That was haunted, which had neither name
Nor form nor voice, nor seem'd it thing externe
Nor alien, but a portion of himself
Passing into a terror which he fear'd
But could not know. Nor ever parted they—
These mates of night—nor could one gaze to where
Another yielded his devour'd heart,
By reason of surrounding shade.

                                    For all
But death were dead. Close-clasping, faith and hope
Lay like twin corses; and the worm was fed
On worship; thought was darken'd; and desire
Watch'd the approaching phantom of decay
With strangling terror in the throat, and died;
Virtue that rotted to one clay with sin;

Love mortal e'en as lust; truth perishing
At pace with falsehood—all were dead, and dead
Was light, and God the first and last of light;—
So dream'd I—

                Open at my waking lay
The page I slept on; but the sudden cry
Of doubt for faith, of darkness for the light,
Of false for true, impure for pure, of frail
For strength, and incomplete for its complete,
And death for life, and earth for Heav'n, and man
For God,—so shook the comfort of my soul—
I turn'd from all the prophet taught, but turn'd
As one that dreams in darkness of the dawn—
But wakes to find no waking of the birds.

ANARCHIA.

THROUGH the mirk air and by the moving main
Slow wand'ring unto ever weirder shade,
That which at first in dubious distance seem'd
The spirit of darkness in the dark astir,
Took form—and from the form a living voice
Awoke, and with strange utterance spake me thus:—

" Art poor or rich? Whichever, heav'n and hell
Will batter thee, their challenged chattell so
In strife to win thee, that whoso doth win

Will win thee soil'd and shapeless. Swear'st by Faith?
Thou art as one that in his hour of need
Should ope some hoarded casket of his house
By nimble thieves unjewell'd, thence to find
It holds but shreds and dust. Is learning thine?
We wrap our robes of knowledge round us so
As hucksters in a masque that feign them kings;
The sudden Unknown plucks us by the sleeve
And laughs to scorn our knowledge of the known.
Dost serve Ambition? Then indeed dost cast
Life's tangible coin into Fame's crucible
To fuse it to thin vapour. Would'st thou free
Thy kind from evil? Then thou art as one
That casts scant water upon flame and feeds
The fire he sought to stifle. For the soul
Of man from sin, too, draws its sustenance
As from the filth about the root the flow'r
Feedeth its blood of beauty. Life is strife:

One plant to gain its verdure starveth ten—
One soul gains heaven by treading ten to hell—
One right inflicts innumerable wrongs—
One pleasure must be fed by many pains—
And evil is the useful foil of good,
And grows a good thereby. Art Venus' slave ?
See, in some mirthful corners of the skies,
The Gods derisive with stop-watch in hand
By seconds note the length of women's loves ;
Love, too, hath grown commercial and doth feign
Romance, as brothels feign reputed trades
To countenance their foulness. Poet art ?
Look to't or, Marsyas-like, thou'lt pay thy skin
For piping—the Apollo of all years
Is match'd against thee ; and the world's too old
To wed the young bride Song, his toothless eld
Espoused to Death already. Would'st by Art,
That which God made in joy remake in pain

Amid mean needs, working by eyes that weep,

And dull His hues of glory to thy grey ?

Then, having caught the shape and slipp'd the soul,

Will life grow fairer for thee ?   Hopest to climb

Beyond thy mortal compass, reaching forth

Vain hands to worlds unsphered in death ?   Behold !

The mountains raise thee so far to the skies,

And then the mountains fail thee.   Say'st to sin—

' I loathe thee,' and to virtue, ' Thee I love ;'

The fates shall mock thee with a changeling bride

To dotage.

    This I speak ; I speak as one

Long dead—sent to the living from the dead

To cry to them they are the fools of dreams,

And that th' immortals make their sport of men,

Not heeding—measuring one end to all—

Careless of agony—laughing at the strife

Of good and ill, and deaf to any prayer,

They lay their laws indiff'rently on all;
Neither with them shall anything avail,
Nor fast of sense, repression of desire,
Nor the ascetic curb of low delight,
Nor service of the higher thoughts that seem
To wrap a golden promise round the heart,
Nor follow'd faith nor duteous deed; and thence
Let thine eye seek henceforth thine eye's delight,
Thy lips their fill of pleasure, thine heart say—
' What better than to eat and drink and die,
And leave no cup untasted by the way,
Ere the dull throat is stifled with thick dust,
And Death is the same God to good and ill;'
And this I speak to thee—I speak as one
Who sought while life was his the height of life—
Soul's power o'er sense, truth's triumph, sin's defeat,
The ways that were the great highways to God;
Who in his proud and passion-troubled youth

Loved beauty and loved danger, and was fed

On daring, but for duty bearded death,

And for a far ideal, like a star,

Forsook the low delights beloved of men,

And strove to keep the stainless soul. But, lo!

The gods make sport of the mad dreams of men,

Who, being beasts, would be as gods." And round

The silence shrank from his strange voice, that cursed

Love, wisdom, worship—things that cheat the heart

And torture; shaking off from him his words

As vipers.

Who, when I essay'd reply,

Withdrew to night. But to my soul I said—

" Be not as those who cleave to doubt, although

One rose to them from death to say ' Believe!'

But rather, though th' arisen from the dead

Should say to thee ' Believe not!' heed him not.

Belief is life, contains its own fulfilment;

All that the soul affirms, the soul shall know ;

And though eternal faith breed transient doubt,

When form is false to soul, when fashions change ;

Though he who on the mount sees face to face

Is sceptic of the golden calves below ;

Yet all true thought shall live, and hope and faith

Are guiding threads that thread the maze of life,

And through the mystery and the mournful dark

Shall lead, and land us in eternal light."

SONNETS.

BEHIND THE VEIL.

To what lone shore or mountain would I go
To catch the murmur from her lip let fall—
If, touch'd by light auroral, life would grow,
Like Memnon in the morning, musical—
In rhythmic revelation uttering all
We agonize to know, while beats in mock
The pulse of being, like a sick-room clock,
Measuring for thought her immemorial thrall;
Some all-including secret of the spheres,
Eaves-dropping at her portal, to have won.
To make man's doubtful guesses and dim fears
Fade as the pale stars fade before the sun,
And earth meet heav'n, as when two mingling meres
Have burst their separant barriers to be one.

RENUNCIATION.

Enough—words, tears, are vain! So let it be.
Alas! what claim had I to love or trust?
I crush my precious pearl of life to dust,
And drown it in the draught I drink to thee.
The after-feast reels from me, and I see
No exit save the portal that unbars
A night beyond the shining of the stars;
Yet if the wintry dark that waiteth me
Leave softer seasons, screen'd from rude annoy,
To nurse thy bloom, this bitterness I bless;
And in the threshold shadow pray no less,
O Sweet, the cup thy happier lips employ,
Of passion's fruitage plunged into the press,
And running thence the ruddy wine of joy.

REJUVENESCENCE.

A SOFT breeze stealing on by lane and lea,
In which all memory of dark days is drown'd—
A sudden vernal glow that seems to be
From lands where death and winter are not found—
A mist of bursting buds on every tree—
A new growth breaking through the hard bare ground,
The pulse of ev'ry plant wakes silently,
And in the wood-bird's pauses stirs a sound—
A sound of resurrection sweet and clear,
From flowing fountains that were frost-bound long,
Comes, falling fresh and happy on the ear
As children's voices in a choral song;
Life's triumph over death is chaunted here—
O, living heart! take courage and be strong.

SUNSET FROM THE COTSWOLDS.

Turning, I gazed o'er the hills' sudden crest,
The whole expanse of western sky to see
Flooded with molten flame tumultuously
By the dissolving orb, whose like bequest
Gave hill and valley each some varying hue—
The fore hills purple, and the far hills blue:
Until the faith arose from thought deprest—
These shows of mortal air, too transient far,
Fade to fulfil themselves in heav'n, and are
Its antitypes of splendour and of rest :
Else were those amphitheatred heights more blest
That, native to the sight, serenely saw—
Though not without a hush of possible awe—
That glory of God descending down the west.

MUSIC FROM THE VALLEY.

Rising in pensive softness, seem'd the strain—
Time, with a trick of sadness on his tongue,
Mourning the lost world, beautiful and young;—
Then burst into a lengthen'd wail; again
With passionate and strong desire was thrill'd—
Yearnings impossible to be fulfill'd,
Immortal language given to mortal pain,—
As though a wand'ring angel, exiled long,
Had learn'd earth's sorrow, yet not lost heav'n's song:
Till, changing to a clear and jubilant blast,
Strong with the triumph over suffering past—
While that full-clarion'd song swell'd far and wide,
Surely some conquering soul stood satisfied
With—and before—the Infinite at last.

THE ITALIAN REVOLUTION.

Italia, O Italia! though thou art
The Magdalene of nations, and hast sold
Thy beauty for the brutal alien's gold,
And play'd with painted smile the hireling's part—
Yet, in thy fall's most fallen hour, for thee
A pardon did the pitying angels keep,
Because thou hadst loved much, and now they weep,
Thee weeping at the Master's feet to see,
And prodigal of precious ointments so—
Spending thy soul in incense at the shrine
Of sorrow, purifying and divine,
Till thou art saint who sinner once did show—
All stains fade from thee, and the holy skies
Sister once more thy consecrated eyes.

EXCELSIOR.

A VALE there is by mist and mirk enshrouded,
From out whereof a mountain doth arise,
Midway, its rugged sides are darkness-clouded;
Higher, its summit shineth to the skies;
And if the mists of error one despise,
Let him take up his pilgrim-staff and wend
Mountwards, and with a daring step ascend;
Nor where the cloud of doubt surrounding lies,
Be faint of heart nor fearful of the end—
But with a forward soul of enterprise
Climb on—and, rising through that nether night,
The lofty summit lands of truth once trod,
Their fields are with perpetual sunshine bright,
And their air holy, being nigh to God.

FAILURE.

He vainly toils who toils to make his life
A Babel-tower whereby to reach the skies;
Aims are confounded, passions fall to strife,
Wisdom is but the folly of the wise;
Ever the soul's deed fails of her emprise—
So is she mock'd and darkness-mazed, and led
To hunger in earth's desert for heav'n's bread.
Bring, sculptor, all the art that in thee lies—
All aid thereto of heart's love and soul's thought,
That so thy brave life-statue may be wrought;
Give all thy days unto the toil, then see
No bright God-image beaming from the stone—
It lies a limbless Dagon overthrown
Upon the bare plains of eternity.

THE INCOMPLETE.

ALL other things drink gladness with their breath—
Sadness, unrest, have in their lives no part—
The bird's wild song, untuned to pain or death,
Springs from a hidden pleasure of the heart;
None empty from life's festal halls depart—
The violet dies not from the woodland side
Till all the soul it hath is satisfied;
But man, into earth's banquet chamber led,
Feeds but on dead-sea fruits, or is not fed—
Or, grasping the pure food too long denied,
Lo! the pale stranger with the shadowy hand
Stands beck'ning to him. From the palace door
He follows—out into the silent land,
Unblest, unsated, to return no more.

ASPIRATION.

O LORD of Hosts, most holy and most strong,
If earthly voices, making pray'r or moan,
Rise where the blessèd forms before Thy throne
Quiver in light as doth the lark in song,
Make haste to hear and answer, be not long;
Thy temples desolated and o'erthrown
Restore ; Thy triune influence make known
To conquer weakness, wilfulness and wrong ;
What power hath made and love hath saved, we pray
That the abiding Paraclete keep whole ;
Our doubts, our sins, our sorrows take away—
Creator, Saviour, and Sustainer be—
That out of all the ways of death the soul
Be drawn through dust and darkness unto Thee.

www.ingramcontent.com/pod-product-compliance
Lightning Source LLC
Chambersburg PA
CBHW030250170426
43202CB00009B/691